DAVID WELLER

How to Stop Procrastinating

Master Your Emotions, Mind, Environment and Time to Conquer Procrastination

Copyright © 2022 by David Weller

All rights reserved. No part of this publication may be reproduced, stored or transmitted in any form or by any means, electronic, mechanical, photocopying, recording, scanning, or otherwise without written permission from the publisher. It is illegal to copy this book, post it to a website, or distribute it by any other means without permission.

First edition

This book was professionally typeset on Reedsy.
Find out more at reedsy.com

To my past self, for not giving up.

Contents

I

Knowledge

1

Introduction

By the end of this book, you will know how to cure your procrastination.

Procrastination is a habit, and like any habit, it can be unlearned and replaced. Here's how: with awareness, self-compassion, and techniques to manage our emotions, mindset, environment, and time. That might sound complex now, but we'll spend the rest of the book unravelling what this means, from understanding why we procrastinate to practical techniques to overcome it.

By the end of this book, you'll have the knowledge, understanding and tools to beat your procrastination.

How do I know this?

Procrastination nearly ruined my life.

I procrastinated and messed up my high school exams. I procrastinated applying for university and took a year out to earn money. I procrastinated again, didn't go to university, and carried on drinking, partying, and spending all the money I earned. In my mid-twenties, I tried studying for a distance-learning degree, but I dropped out after a year because of procrastination.

I knew I was pretty intelligent, but I couldn't beat procrastination.

I tried reading books, and articles, asking friends, changing habits, everything I could think of. The pattern was always the same - incredible enthusiasm when I started a new project, then procrastination and giving up after two or three weeks. I had a succession of crap jobs in different cities until I eventually ran away so hard that I ended up teaching English in the middle of China.

Procrastination was stealing my life.

So what changed? I'll tell you in a minute.

Short, simple, effective.

This is a short book.

If you're worried about procrastination, you want to start fixing it immediately and not spend hours reading unnecessary details. That's why this book is concise, illustrated, and will help you get started straight away.

Here's the plan:

Section 1 - Knowledge

The first section, 'Knowledge' will provide you with the what, why, and how of procrastination. What it is, what we know about it (scientifically speaking), and how it works. This may seem unnecessary, but don't skip it - the better you know your enemy, the easier you'll be able to overcome it.

Chapter 2

Will show you you're not alone in procrastinating. Some of human history's most famous, prolific minds have struggled like you. Draw courage from seeing familiar names of people who have overcome procrastination.

Chapter 3

Looks at the price of procrastination. Spoiler: it's worse than you think. Procrastination harms individuals and society so much that it deserves to be called evil.

Chapter 4

Is where we discover the root cause of procrastination and identify our true enemy.

Chapter 5

Looks at the emotions we feel as we procrastinate or how procrastination expresses itself through us. We must thoroughly understand the major and minor effects to combat them.

Chapter 6

This chapter looks at procrastination on a scale, from mild to severe, and helps you understand where you are in your journey.

Chapter 7

Procrastination shows in many different ways, and this chapter looks at all the symptoms of procrastination you might recognize in yourself and others.

Section 2 - Concepts

This section will cover the most important principles and concepts (or mindsets) that you should read and 'install' into your mind ready to tackle your procrastination. By understanding how our minds work, you'll be able to see your situation and actions in a different perspective. I'm sure you've seen that famous image that if you look at it one way, it's an old lady, and if you look at it a different way, it's a rabbit - this section will also expand and change the way you understand and see yourself.

Section 3 - Techniques

Contains the practical knowledge you'll need to get to procrastination zero.

Chapter 8

Outlines the framework we'll be using to combat procrastination.

Chapters 9-12

Look at each area of the techniques you'll use. They're grouped broadly into four buckets - emotions, mindset, environment, and time.

So what happened?

To finish my earlier story:

Luckily, I fell in with a great crowd of people looking to improve their teaching and become the best they could be. I realized I'd had enough and desperately started researching how to overcome what felt like a debilitating disease.

Instead of feel-good self-help books, I started to read scientific literature. Instead of wishing for the best, I started testing these scientific concepts on myself and seeing what worked. Instead of hiding and feeling sorry for myself, I started competing with my peers to try new things and learn more.

The result?

Since I've regularly started applying these techniques, I've completed a postgraduate diploma and a master's degree in teaching, been promoted multiple times, changed careers, created a successful blog, and written three books (this is the fourth).

While I fell off the wagon a few times, with this new understanding and these techniques, I knew how to restart and dared to do so. Being a procrastinator is a little like being an addict. Even with good habits, it's easy to fall off the wagon during times of unusual stress. We're only human. But with the knowledge and skills in this book, you'll know you'll be able to recover.

How to use this book

As well as reading, you'll need to act. You won't be able to solve your procrastination just by skimming through this book!

To start your journey, as you read, at the end of each chapter will be questions for you and space to write your answers. As you read each, take the time to relax, pause, think, and write your answer. In some cases, the answer may flash instantly in your mind. For other questions, you might need to ask yourself 'why is this the case' a few times to get past a superficial answer. Example tk.

I know you'll be tempted to skip over answering these questions (I would be too!), but trust me -the more you interact with this book, the more likely you are to succeed. If you simply skim over these you won't get the same benefit. As we'll see in chapter tk, the deeper we think and process information, the more likely that the information will be learned, and the bigger the change it'll have on our minds and actions.

Get started

It's time to start your journey!

as you read and apply the lessons in this book, you'll improve your ability to resist procrastinating and get things done. If you use the knowledge, concepts, and techniques consistently, you'll get to zero procrastination.

It's an ongoing battle that'll become easier and more manageable. If you have a bad day or week, there is no need to chastise yourself; keep moving forward. As the famous philosopher, Seneca said, don't waste your life - don't let life pass you by without seeing what you're capable of doing.

Make time to read the rest of this book—schedule time on your calendar. Sit down with a pencil, ready to answer the questions, and make notes when something resonates with you. Leave this book on the counter or somewhere you'll see it daily. Start to practice, and let your results motivate you more than I ever could.

It's time to escape the cycle of endless procrastination.

Procrastinate
Feel guilty

2

You're Not Alone

First, understand that you are not alone.

Most people experience procrastination to some degree, with one study finding that the average person procrastinates for a total of 55 days per year[1] (that's altogether, not on one project!).

Procrastination affects our productivity, health, wealth, and mental well-being, with one study finding that 94% of people reported that procrastination negatively affects their happiness[2].

In my experience, intelligent people seem to suffer from procrastination more. I believe this is because the wiser you are, the faster you can visualize what the task will require, and the quicker you'll become bored.

Procrastinators feel they are the only ones who procrastinate and suffer in silence. You can change, so don't be hard on yourself.

Procrastination isn't a new phenomenon. People have procrastinated since before people were people. Here's a list of people who procrastinated throughout history yet still became famous.

4 BC

Demosthenes, a Greek orator, shaves half his head, so he must stay indoors and practice his speeches or face public humiliation.

400s AD

St Augustine of Hippo offers a prayer to help him overcome the lewd temptations he procrastinates from solving - "Grant me chastity and continence—but not yet."

1490s AD

Leonardo da Vinci takes sixteen years to finish his masterpiece 'The Mona Lisa'. He then finishes his painting 'The Last Supper' in just three years when a wealthy patron threatens to withdraw his funding.

1751 AD

Samuel Johnson, the creator of the first dictionary, procrastinates on writing an article about procrastination, finishing at a friend's house while the publisher's delivery boy waits outside.

1787 AD

Mozart writes the overture to his opera 'Don Giovanni' the night before the premiere. The ink is still wet on copies of the sheet music as the opera starts.

1830 AD

Victor Hugo strips naked and orders his servant not to return his clothes until a specific time. He's spent a year procrastinating while writing 'The Hunchback of Notre Dame'.

1850 AD

Herman Melville's wife chains him to his desk daily so he can finish his novel, 'Moby Dick'.

1800s AD

Samuel Taylor Coleridge frequently chooses smoking opium over writing poetry. It was later said "his existence became a never-ending squalor of procrastination, excuses, lies, debts, degradation, failure."

1935 AD

Frank Lloyd Wright designs his most famous house in two hours. Why? His client says he's dropping by to see the 'nearly finished' plans, which Wright hadn't started.

1970 AD

Hunter S Thompson rips out pages of his scribbled notebook and gives them to a waiting courier to make a deadline. It becomes his famous piece, 'The Kentucky Derby is Decadent and Depraved'.

1984 AD

Douglas Adams is locked in a hotel suite with his editor for three weeks to finish his book 'So Long, and Thanks for All the Fish'.

There would be more people on this list, but guess what? They procrastinated.

The people above were lucky and succeeded despite their procrastination. They often had strong support networks or periods of intense pressure, which helped temporarily overcome their procrastination.

Imagine how many procrastinators didn't have their luck and passed on without leaving their mark on history.

Start a task

I'll start tomorrow

I'll start soon

I've still got time

Can I get out of it?

What's wrong with me?

I'm in so much trouble

"I'll never procrastinate again!"

Finish a task (or not!)

3

The Price of Procrastination

"The cost of procrastination is the life you could've lived."
- Anonymous.

Procrastination can ruin your life.

Most people don't realize just how detrimental procrastination can be. A short delay here and there can be easily justified and seems like nothing to worry about.

But over time, the effects of procrastination compound, and we miss out not just on opportunities but on further opportunities they would have brought.

Compound interest is sometimes called the world's eighth wonder, and Albert Einstein called it "the most powerful force in the universe." This is a beautiful thing in finance, where we can invest our money to make money (interest) and then use the interest to make even more money. Our wealth can grow exponentially over time.

However, opportunities can also compound positively in life, and missed opportunities compound negatively. Missed opportunities to build wealth, develop relationships and enjoy life multiply exponentially.

As the quotation at the start of this chapter implies, the price of procrastination is our best potential life. All the things you could be, do, or have are just possibilities. If you put forward consistent effort, you can reach your best life. If you procrastinate, you'll have a life full of regrets and wondering 'what could have been'.

In fact, the negative impact of procrastination goes even deeper than this and can be divided into two sides: internal costs and external consequences. Internal costs are how our feelings process our procrastination and are affected. External consequences are how the world reflects our procrastination back at us by denying our potential.

Procrastination is a thief, not just of time, but of potential and positivity.

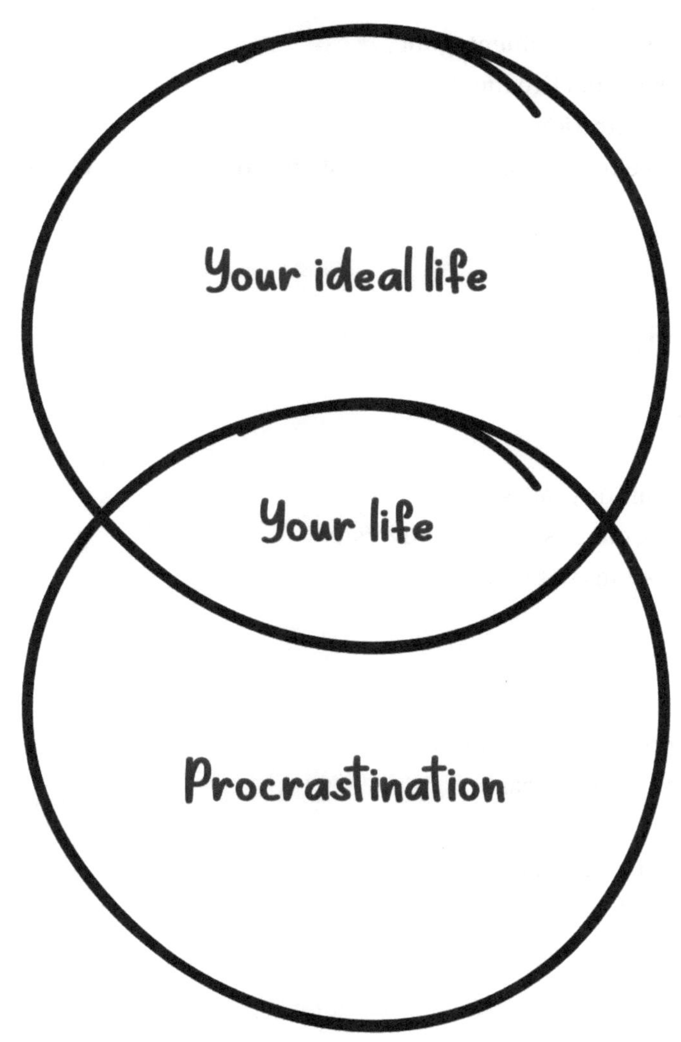
Your ideal life
Your life
Procrastination

Possible Internal Costs

- Self-criticism and low self-image
- Anxiety, fear, dread
- Shame, embarrassment, guilt
- Depression and tiredness
- Anger, frustration, panic
- Stress, feeling harassed, feeling rushed and out of control.

Possible External Consequences

Academic

- Low or failing grades[3].
- Dropping out of school or university.
- Qualifications not obtained.

Career

- Lost promotion opportunities.[4]
- Missed salary increases.[5]
- Conflict with management.
- Being made redundant.
- Being fired.

Wealth

- Less money saved.
- Fewer investments.
- Lower credit rating.
- Higher chance of fines and penalties.

- Higher consumer debt[6].

Health

- Decreased fitness
- More severe impact of bad health.
- Higher chance of late diagnosis.
- Higher chance of illness.
- Higher chance of high blood pressure and heart disease.

Relationships

- Less chance of meeting a partner.
- Conflict with your partner.
- Higher chance of separation from your partner.
- Higher chance of loneliness

In one area, procrastination is bad. If you procrastinate in all areas, imagine how bad it would be!

It is true that procrastination steals potential. Individually it's terrible, but think how much the world could've achieved if everyone had lived up to their potential!

There's a positive side, though - the good compounds once we stop procrastinating. We can harness the same force of compounding, but for good. And that's what we'll look at now.

4

The Roots of Procrastination

"While we waste our time hesitating and postponing, life is slipping away."
— Seneca

Procrastination is a complex problem with many variables affecting it. At its root, though, procrastination is a problem with managing our emotions[7].

Our emotions influence our thinking and behavior much more than our intellect. As procrastinators, we have trouble regulating our feelings - when we're feeling anxious or in a bad mood, we tend to wait until things are better before taking action.

Procrastination is also linked with a lack of temporal thinking and self-control[8]. The ability to envision the future—thinking about time and planning for the long-term—is linked with self-control. People who are good at this type of thinking tend to be more successful in life; those who struggle with temporal thinking are more likely to procrastinate.

It's not that you are lazy. There are many reasons why people procrastinate, and it's essential to identify the underlying causes so we can address them directly.

Try and remember the first few times you procrastinated. What happened? Most likely, you felt pressure, worried, procrastinated, felt relieved (that you finished or it wasn't too difficult).

The solution is working with our emotions. Everyone has a different way of expressing their procrastination, and so there will be different specific techniques (and blends of techniques) that we can use to stop procrastinating.

We need to get our emotions on our side and not working against us. The next chapter will look at how our emotions manifest – see which scenarios sound like you!

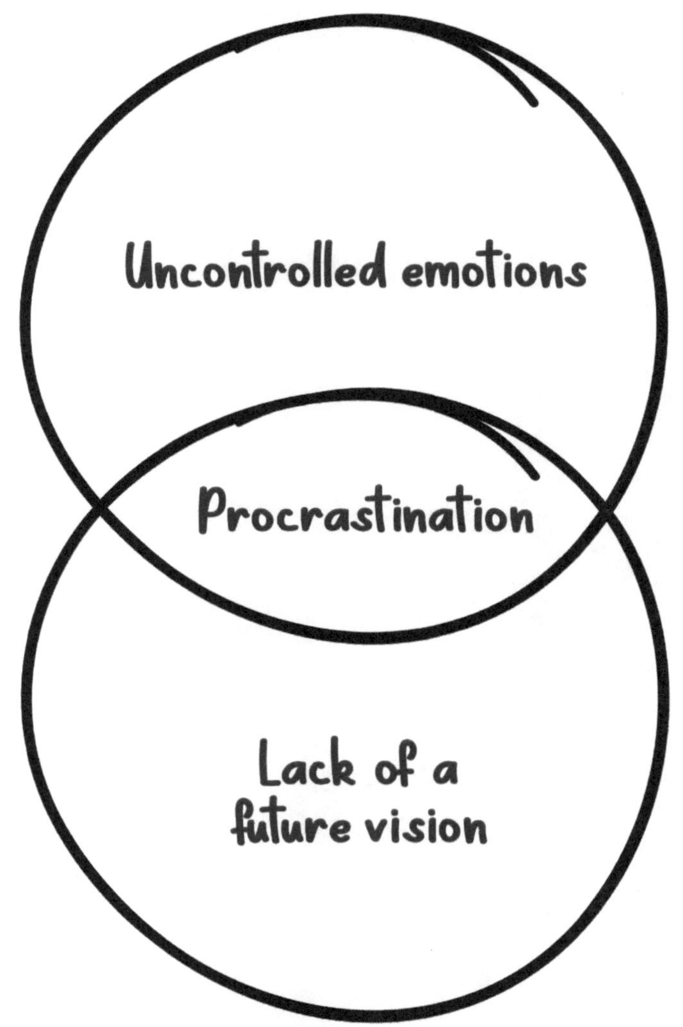
Uncontrolled emotions
Procrastination
Lack of a
future vision

5

Emotions Running Wild

We've found that emotions are the root of our procrastination - but which emotions, and how do they manifest?

The following is a guide to the emotions we feel when we procrastinate. As you read through, notice which you feel most affects you. Identifying and naming the emotion can help you better overcome it, as it'll be easier to choose which techniques to use from section two of this book.

Anxiety or fear

Now, as humans, we're hardwired to feel fear. There are many different reasons we feel fear, but it is a survival mechanism that has served us and our ancestors for untold generations.

The problem is, with our relatively comfortable modern standard of living, our fear mechanisms are hijacked by concerns that aren't life-threatening. Failing a task can raise specters in our minds, from the childhood trauma of overbearing parents to the worst things that could happen if we fail, all crowded into our minds. This is known as 'catastrophizing', and is a cognitive distortion where our brains leap to visualize the worst possible outcome, further increasing our fear of failure.

We can also attach our self-worth to the successful outcomes of tasks, which makes the possibility of failure a fearful event.One model suggests that there are five basic fears and that all our other fears arise from these or are combinations of these.

We fear extinction

This is a fear of death, but also the fear of not being around anymore – of not seeing life carry on, of seeing friends and family, or them not being able to see you. This one isn't often a cause of procrastination.

We fear mutilation

Thankfully not usually a prompt for procrastination either, this is a fear of not being able to use your body as it was designed. It also is a cause of fears related to animals, spiders, etc.

We fear the loss of autonomy

We fear being controlled, either physically or mentally, or a loss of control. Physically this can lead to fears like claustrophobia, and mentally it can lead to issues in relationships. Fear of commitment can also arise from this fear.

We fear separation

This covers the fears of being abandoned, being rejected, and becoming a non-person – basically not being respected or valued by others.This includes the fear of others judging us and finding us inferior or lesser than our perception of ourselves. Humans are tribal creatures[9], and to be considered lesser in a tribe has consequences – from mating rights to perhaps exile and death. Even to this day, the lingering fear is a strong one.

Fears of leaving our comfort zone and fear of success also can arise from this fundamental fear, as can the more modern 'fear of missing out'. Even though we all have fears, it's important to remember that failure doesn't always mean that one will never succeed. There are times when anxiety can sneak up on us and prevent us from finishing projects. The key to getting back on track is identifying the reasons we procrastinate and taking the necessary steps to resolve them.

We fear ego-death

By ego-death, we mean losing our sense of self or of our constructed identity. It's a fear of change, of shame or humiliation, or anything else that threatens to change what we think of ourselves.

Feel a lack of purpose

Lack of purpose can lead to a lack of goals, which leads to apathy and procrastination. This is because many of us don't know our purpose in life, or we have let it dwindle and die over time, perhaps due to distraction and busyness.

It could also be that our purpose is not a good match for who we really are.

Perhaps it was set long ago by someone else (usually well-meaning parents). We may have been raised with the idea that our goal is to achieve certain things at all costs, which can lead to stress.

A lack of purpose leads to a lack of drive, which significantly contributes to procrastination.[10]

Feeling bored

In the scientific literature, procrastinating because you're bored is known as 'task aversion,' According to one meta-analysis[11], those who consider a task boring are more likely to procrastinate on it.

From my experience, the more intelligent a person is, the faster they're likely to become bored and, therefore, more likely to procrastinate. An intelligent person can quickly analyze a task, visualize the steps involved, see the repetitive nature and envision how long it will take, and think of things they'd rather do with that time.

Feeling confused or overwhelmed

Confusion is when we're unsure what to do or how to do it. This could come from not taking the time to think through a task, not being trained well enough, or a lack of experience with insufficient guidance.

Feeling overwhelmed is where you might know what to do but have too much coming at you too fast to process. The neuroscientific term for this is 'cognitive overload', which is when our brains become overloaded with information.

Cognitive overload can happen with tasks that are new to you (there's often lots to think about and remember) or tasks that you know how to do but at an increased speed.

Both confusion and overwhelm can lead to procrastination.

Feeling unmotivated

Feeling unmotivated to do a task can occur for a few reasons. It could be a general lack of motivation, when we don't feel like doing anything. This type can be caused by low energy, hunger, a lack of sleep, tiredness from a long day, or similar.

Feeling unmotivated about a particular task is usually an issue with how we see the task itself. Either we haven't thought through the task and are confused about exactly what to do, or feeling reluctant to start given the size of the task.

Motivation can vary from the beginning of the task to the end of it. We can start by feeling highly motivated, only to become demotivated when we realize it will take longer than expected. Or we might feel unmotivated at the beginning but then get into the 'flow' of the task, find it enjoyable, and become motivated.

Feeling distracted

When we're feeling one or more of the emotions we've looked at, it becomes much more likely that we'll be easily distracted.

Of course, it's much easier to feel distracted in a cluttered and messy environment, not to mention it's harder to concentrate.

Our phones are also a primary cause of distraction. Anything that interrupts our focus as we do a task is likely to cause distraction, and our phone notifications are a prime example of this.

Sometimes our phone notifications don't even need to be on – one study found that simply being able to see your phone while you work increases the chances of procrastination[12].

Feeling disconnected

A very similar feeling to being unmotivated, but this is more that you're finding it hard to connect your life and actions to tangible outcomes.

You feel disconnected from your current self and are unsure why you're doing what you are. Completing tasks seems like a waste of time, and when you don't associate a task with a high-level goal, it increases your tendency to procrastinate.[13]

Underlying issues

Procrastination can also be a symptom of an underlying cause, such as ADHD or depression[14]. You should seek professional advice if you think this may be the case.

Summary

So many emotions can cause procrastination that it seems we have an army facing us. The good news is that we can turn our procrastination around! The first step is to acknowledge the emotions that are holding us back. Once we recognize what's going on, it's time to take small steps toward our goals and confidently move forward.

6

Types of Procrastination

There are several types of procrastination, according to one cluster analysis[15]. They are:

- Mild, average, and severe
- Acute and chronic
- Anxious and hedonistic
- Active and passive
- Domain-specific

Mild, average, and severe procrastination

Think of this as a scale running from mild to awful.

It's a subjective scale, and each person might rate their procrastination differently. It's as you would expect - if you describe yourself as a mild procrastinator, you don't procrastinate often. Average would be someone who procrastinates often, and severe would be so often that it leads to significant stress and impact on their life (sometimes called pathological procrastination).

You might also rate yourself at different levels in different situations, environments, or different types of tasks.

Acute and chronic procrastination

Acute procrastination is short-term, and chronic is long-term.

Acute procrastination might happen when you're trying to write an essay, prepare a report, or for any stressful event. It's usually focused on a specific task and is relatively short-term (until it is completed).

Chronic procrastination refers to the habitual delay in completing tasks. It's present for a wide variety of tasks and continues over time. To some, it might seem that this type of procrastination happens frequently enough that it seems to have become part of that person's personality.

Anxious and hedonistic procrastination

Anxious procrastination is delaying tasks even though you want to work on them. For example, you're desperate to finish an essay or presentation, you open the file on your computer, and yet you're irresistibly drawn to opening your browser and checking your social media.

Hedonistic procrastination is choosing to delay tasks to spend time having fun. It's a more conscious choice to delay – perhaps your task has a deadline that's far in the future, so you decide to treat yourself to some time off.

Active and passive procrastination

Sometimes known as positive and negative procrastination, it divides procrastination into two types:

- Active = deliberate delay, which leads to a positive result
- Passive = involuntary delay, which leads to a negative result

Active procrastination might involve deliberately waiting until the day before a deadline, so you'll work faster and harder. A passive procrastinator might want to do the same task but feel unable to start until the final day (or they might miss the deadline altogether!).

Domain-specific procrastination

This is procrastination for a specific area of your life or work.

Cal Newport coined the term in his book How to Win at College. He describes it as "getting distracted by activities that are related to your goal but not directly related to it." These activities can include reading books on a topic that's relevant to your work, attending seminars and conferences on topics that interest you, or even spending time on social media sites like Facebook and Twitter.

There are three well-known domains:

Academic procrastination

is the tendency to delay studying, reading, and writing assignments until the day they're due. It's a common problem for students in all subject areas, but it can be especially detrimental to those in STEM fields.

Workplace procrastination

involves putting off work to do more enjoyable tasks such as socializing, relaxing, or surfing the web. People may also skip out on meetings or other professional obligations to do less critical tasks.

Bedtime procrastination

Is when people put off going to bed because they don't want their fun time to end. Also known as 'revenge bedtime procrastination', this can lead to poor sleep quality and excessive daytime drowsiness.

Did you recognize yourself in any of these descriptions? What kind of procrastinator are you?

7

How We Procrastinate

"That's a problem for future Homer. Man, I don't envy that guy." - Homer Simpson

This leads to a circle of procrastination. [line diagram tk]

We've now seen that the root cause is our emotions and temporal thinking. We've seen which emotions it causes and the types of procrastination - now, let's look at how procrastination can manifest itself for you.

Some procrastination is obvious - we don't get stuff done.

In moderation, it seems OK. We get most of our tasks done. But then it starts to get worse. The report goes unwritten, the tap still leaks, the book goes unwritten, the paints stay in the pot, and the code goes unwritten. However, some forms of procrastination are cunning, and they disguise themselves.

The first step to fighting procrastination is becoming aware of it in all its forms. These forms are the techniques that procrastination uses against us and the warning signs we should look for in ourselves.

How many do you recognize?

We avoid

We don't do the thing. We play computer games instead of writing an essay. We wait until the last minute to do the thing (or we simply don't do it at all). In extreme cases, this is known as avoidance coping and can lead to damaging psychological consequences.

We deny

We tell ourselves that we don't have to do the thing. It's not our job to do it, it's not needed for our course of study, or it's optional, so we don't really have to do it. We can get away with ignoring it.

We trivialize

We lie to ourselves (and others) that what we want to do isn't actually that important. As it's unimportant, we don't have to do it and can do something more fun. This is common with tasks that are important for the long-term but not urgent (things like exercising, professional development, or a faraway essay deadline).

We get distracted

We completely forget our task as we've been seduced by something entirely—the feeling when you search online for something only to spend two hours watching videos. You didn't make a conscious decision - it just happened.

We compare

We make ourselves feel better by comparing how much someone else hasn't done to how much we haven't done. We know this is a false comparison deep in our hearts, but it soothes our minds and allows us to procrastinate guilt-free.

We boast

We show off what we have achieved, ignoring what we could've or should've done in the meantime.

We blame

We convince ourselves that forces beyond our control are responsible for stopping us. Some rationalizations are desperate - a tiny bit of rain seems like a good reason not to take the trash out or go for a run. Or we blame other people - we can't start the essay because a friend didn't give us the notes he promised.

We mock

We mock ourselves (in front of others and alone) to use humor to relieve our internal pressure. When we laugh, it relieves stress, and the psychological pressure that's been building is relieved[16]. That relief allows us mental space to procrastinate once more without feeling guilty.

We get revenge

Revenge bedtime procrastination is when we delay going to sleep to feel more in control[17]. It's usually triggered by not having much time because of a busy schedule. So to give us time to enjoy our lives, have fun, and feel more in control, we 'get revenge' on our future selves. We know we'll wake up tired with no energy, but it doesn't seem to matter in the moment.

We work on lesser tasks

Known as productive procrastination, we do work - just not the work we should be doing. Tidy the house instead of writing an essay. Organize our sock drawer instead of preparing a presentation. My house has never been cleaner and tidier than when I was writing my master's dissertation.

We talk

Instead of working on a project, we tell our friends about it. Then our family. Then anyone who'll listen. If you're always telling someone what you're going to do and not what you've done, you're most likely using it as a way to procrastinate.

One study[18] showed the reduction in motivation that comes from telling our friends our plans - this is because our brain feels the rush of dopamine we get from vividly imagining a successful outcome, removing the anticipated reward we'd get from actually finishing.

A rule of thumb: tell what you've done, not what you're going to do.

We plan

Planning is exciting! We get the dopamine rush from thinking about a new project and how extraordinary success will feel. This is similar to the 'We Talk' above, except by planning, we're telling ourselves how good it'll be to succeed. So we dive in and plan

Planning is needed, but when it gets in the way of starting, it's procrastination behavior.

We help

We offer our help to friends, then use it as an excuse not to work on ourselves. This is a seductive type of procrastination, as we label ourselves as kind, caring people for helping others so much, but then we neglect ourselves and our dreams in the process.

A balance is essential - we can balance being caring with caring about ourselves.

II

Concepts

8

Concept #1: Emotions

As we saw in chapter 4, procrastination develops from problems with regulating and managing our emotions.

Another way to think of this is that procrastination is a solution to the emotional challenges we've been having. There's nothing wrong with us because we procrastinate, simply procrastination is a side effect of our emotional regulation.

So learning the emotional techniques in the next section will help, but there's a baseline mindset that we need to adopt before we start. This is because learning to overcome procrastination isn't just a technical process. We can't simply learn a few tricks and expect everything to be fixed instantly. We need to go deeper into our emotions and change how we perceive ourselves.

Forgiveness

First of all, forgiveness - we must forgive ourselves for procrastinating in the past. Often we linger on our mistakes, on how much we could have achieved, or how our lives would've been different if we hadn't procrastinated and had achieved the goals we set out to.

But it doesn't serve any purpose to do so. We can't change the past, and it won't do us any good to wallow in past mistakes. Why would we keep kicking ourselves for what's past? Think of it like this - keeping your mind fixed on old mistakes is itself a form of procrastination.

Kindness

While forgiveness is aimed at our pasts, kindness is aimed at ourselves in the present. You need to be kind to yourself as you go through this process of change.

During the process, it's inevitable that you'll make mistakes, fall off the wagon, and have to start over. Some days will go really well, and you'll feel completely in control, and others will feel like a trainwreck. Some days you'll want to write off completely by lunchtime, and want to curl up on the sofa and ignore the world.

That's normal, and it's OK. Be patient with yourself, understand that it will take time, and take the next step. Not giving up is more important than 100% consistency.

Self-esteem

Right now, you're probably not feeling good about yourself or your ability to complete tasks. That's because completing tasks builds confidence and self-esteem, while procrastinating lowers them.

You'll notice that as you start to complete more tasks in a day (or procrastinate less), you'll feel better about yourself, and pride in your accomplishment (self-esteem) and you'll feel better about your ability to do the same or better in the future, because you've proven to yourself that you're capable (your confidence).

Remember these feelings next time you're struggling.

9

Concept #2: Decisions

Think of each day as a series of decisions. Every day is a stream of decisions that you make, either consciously or not. Do you choose to have a cup of coffee now, or later? Do you pull your phone out your pocket or not? Do you open an app to waste time or not? Do you switch over to another browser tab to check the news or not?

Have you ever read a 'choose your own adventure' book? You know, the ones where you read then choose - option A, go to page 20; option B, page 32. As a kid, I loved them, but I always cheated. I used my thumb as a bookmark to flip back if my decision had terrible consequences.

Every day is a 'choose your own adventure', and every decision changes the outcome you'll get at the end of the day. But now, there's no cheating - you can't turn back after a poor decision, time has already gone by. Another name for this is a 'decision tree'. You start from the same place, but there are countless paths to get through a day.

You build your day on thousands of decisions. Some you make consciously, some you inherit from your training, and some reflect your character. Unconscious habits will rule your life if you don't make conscious decisions. So many people get to the end of the day and wonder what on earth happened, and where the day went.

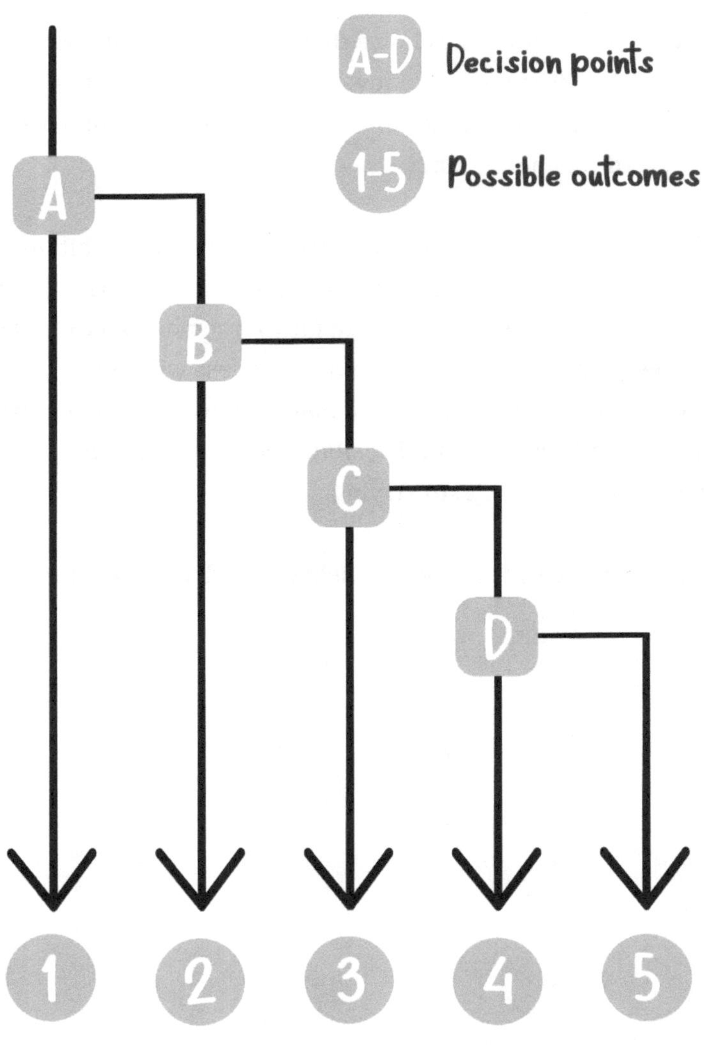
A-D Decision points
1-5 Possible outcomes
A
B
C
D
1
2
3
4
5

The first step to overcoming procrastination and getting the outcomes you want is becoming aware of the moments you're making decisions, especially when you unconsciously procrastinate.

The second step is making the choice that future you would be proud of, in those moments of awareness. What would the 'you' in eight hours think of your choice? Would they be grateful? Or would they regret and feel remorse that they wasted yet another day?

The third step is to practice this consistently and make it a habit. At first, you might forget dozens of times and only remember once or twice daily. That's OK, keep trying. The next day you might only remember once or twice more, that's OK, keep trying. Eventually, your awareness will raise, and you'll be able to have a moment of awareness to make a conscious choice about what you want to do and control your decisions. Don't forget to forgive yourself when you mess up, but don't stop trying.

The techniques in the last section will help you with this even further.

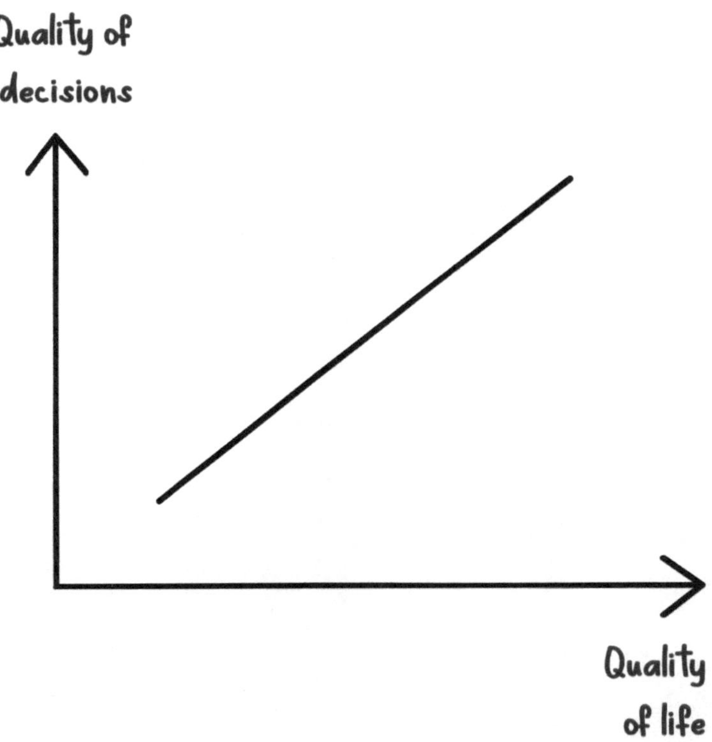
Quality of decisions
Quality of life

•

10

Concept #3: Thinking

Feeling overwhelmed and confused is a common trigger for procrastination. *Cognitive load theory* is the scientific name for how we manage the amount of information (and information overload). It explains how we process and remember information and how too much (or too complex) information harms learning.

Cognitive load theory came from research into problem-solving[19]. It showed that working memory has a limited capacity and described the relationship between working and long-term memory.

As you receive information, the senses pass some data to your working memory, while it ignores a lot (you can't process and remember every tiny detail of what you see and hear!). Your working memory might rehearse the information for clarity (or not), and then it's processed (or encoded) into your long-term memory. The same is true, but in reverse, when you recall information you want to use. Your working memory acts like a gatekeeper, as it works hard to filter all the information it receives and decides which to keep.

Unfortunately, sensory and working memory aren't that large and can become overwhelmed with information. When this happens, we start to feel stressed, anxious, and frustrated - this is often the point when we'll throw up our hands, pick up our phone, and start scrolling on social media to take a break.

So what does this mean for us in daily life?

It means that when you feel overwhelmed, pause instead of checking out and switching from a task to a procrastination activity. Think back to the last chapter, on decisions, and take a moment of awareness. You might choose to take a five-minute break, walk around the block, do something physically active, or meditate. Do whatever helps you clear your mind.

When you go back to the task, start breaking it down into smaller and smaller chunks.

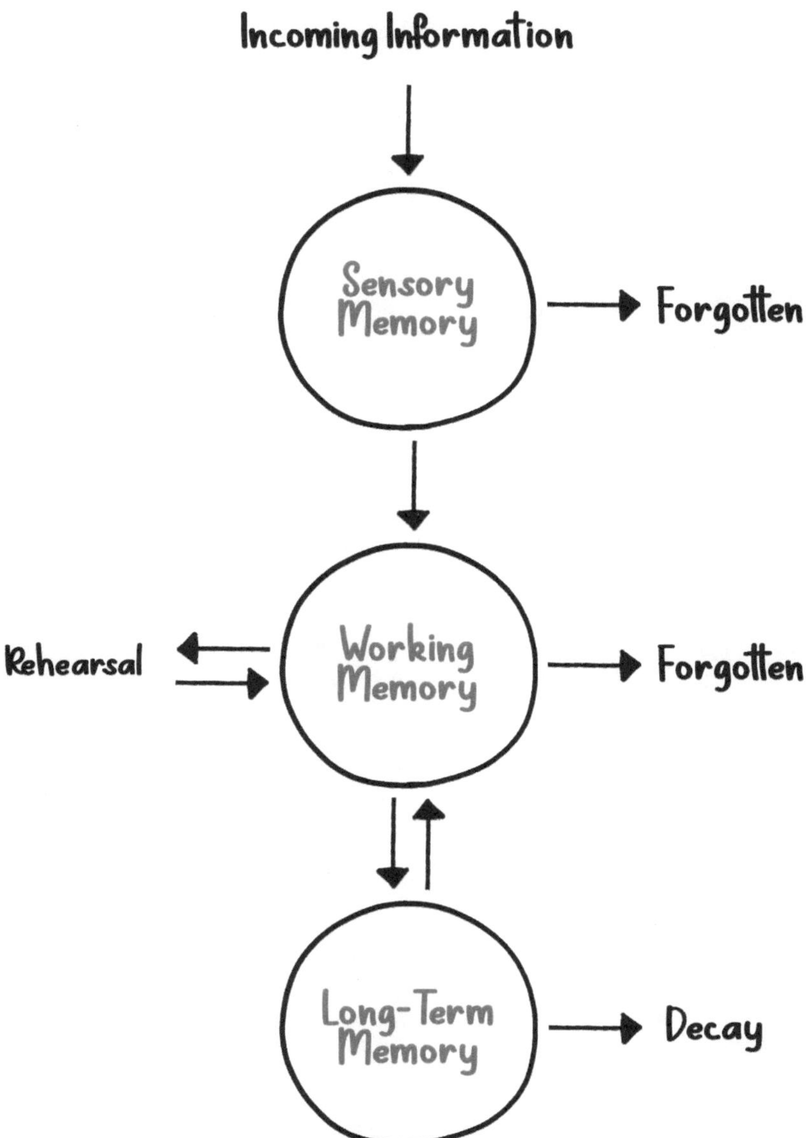
Incoming Information
Sensory Memory
Forgotten
Rehearsal
Working Memory
Forgotten
Long-Term Memory
Decay

11

Concept #4: Time & Stress Distortion

Be aware that procrastination plays tricks with our perceptions and our emotions.

The first trick is playing around with our anxiety levels when we think about what we want to get done. The closer we come to starting a task, the more anxious we feel. All of the fear, guilt, and anxiety surge, causing us to create excuses and procrastinate once again. We fear that the task will be too hard, or we won't know what to do

Yet a strange thing happens once we actually start - our negative emotions evaporate. All that worry and fear disappears as we start to make progress. This is a really good concept to remember to combat that feeling the next time this happens.

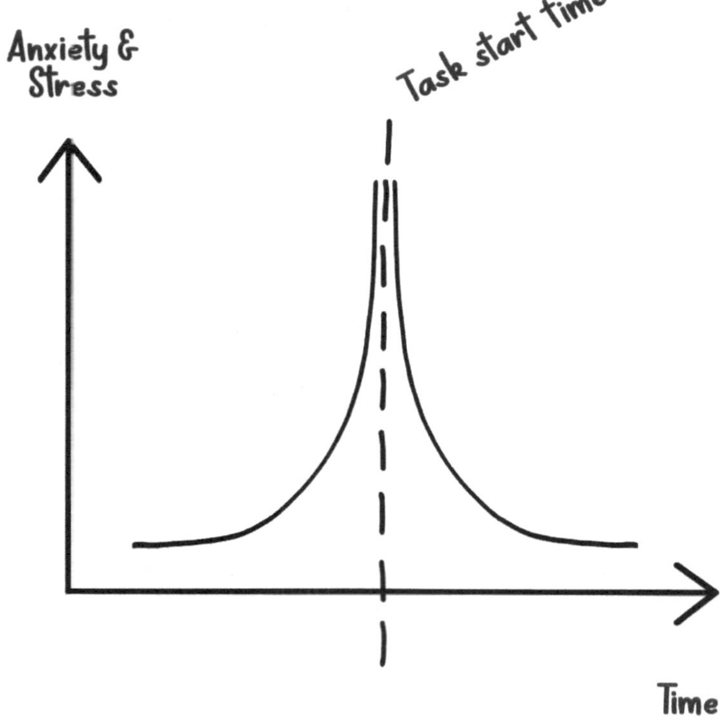
Anxiety &
Stress
Task start time
Time

The same thing happens with our perception of time when we think ahead to how long a task will take. One of two things happens:

1. We think the task will take forever, and so we don't want to start such a seemingly huge project without mentally preparing
2. We think the task will be so short that we could do it at any time, causing us to procrastinate as there's no hurry to do it immediately.

Yet once we start work on the task, we usually realise the opposite is true - huge tasks seem more manageable than we anticipated (hurrah!), but small tasks expand in scope (boo!). What's happened is that procrastination has used whichever method it can to trick us into delaying our work. Which we'll talk more about in the next chapter.

III

Techniques

12

Framework & Techniques

Procrastination is complex.

We've discussed different types of procrastination, reasons why we procrastinate, and the range of emotions that fuel procrastination. With so much variation in causes and symptoms, is it any wonder that there are no simple, one-size fits all solutions?

When we look at why we procrastinate, We can categorize the reasons we procrastinate into a hierarchy of most to least impactful. At the core, as we've discovered, emotions are the fundamental reason that we procrastinate. So emotional management techniques will therefore have the most significant impact on our procrastination.

A Hierarchy of Techniques

The techniques we'll be using can be organized into broad groups based on what kind of techniques they are. These technique groups are:

- Emotional
- Mindset

- Environmental (physical and digital)
- Time

We can then place groups in a hierarchy based on how close they are to the root cause of procrastination. The order will look like this, with emotional techniques being closest to the cause of procrastination:

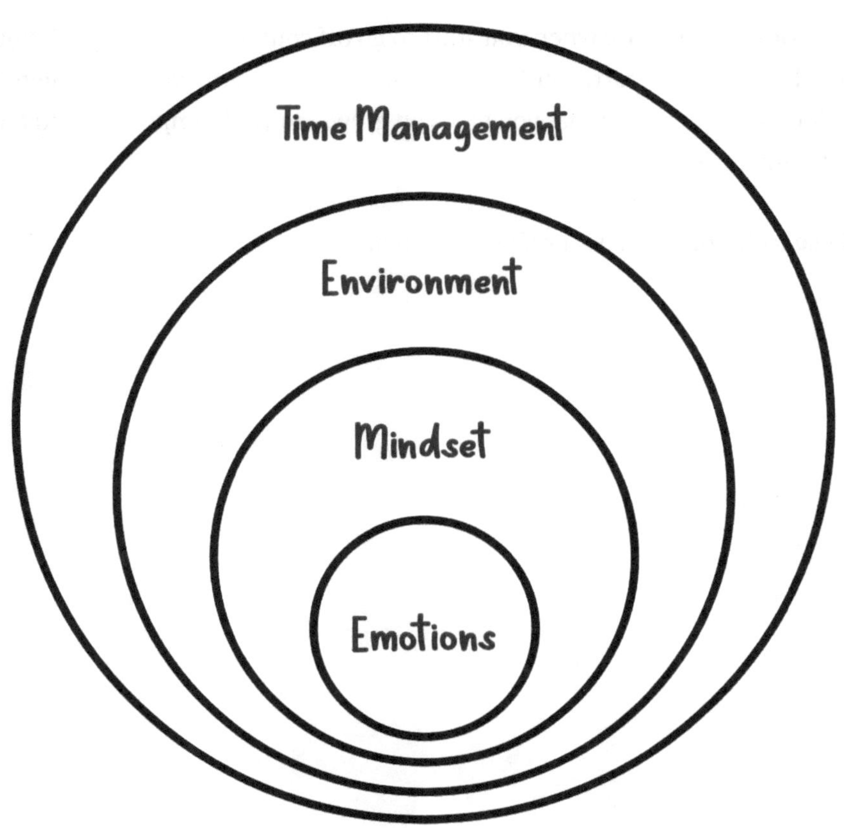
Time Management
Environment
Mindset
Emotions

Applying the Techniques

Use these techniques with awareness. Be aware of the techniques that seem uncomfortable for you to do - these might be the ones that are the most beneficial to you.

Start slowly. Be aware when you start to go off course. Keep a journal. You'll find that once you start, you'll build positive momentum, which will help you maintain the journey. What you focus on grows, so you'll improve if you focus on taking action.

These techniques will work if you use them.

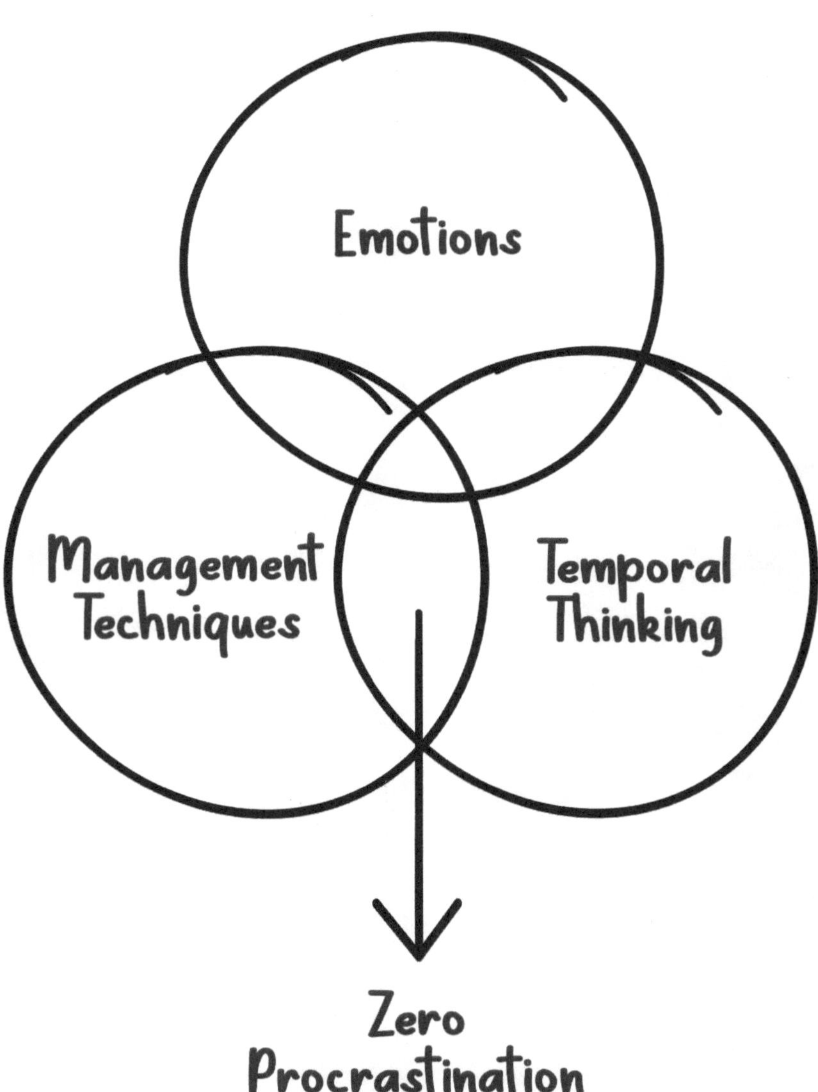
Emotions
Management Techniques
Temporal Thinking
Zero Procrastination

•

13

Emotional Management Techniques

Even being aware that procrastination is an emotional issue can help.

You can stop beating yourself up for thinking you're being lazy, stupid, or have terrible time management. Now that we know we're not lazy, we can start addressing the fundamental issue of managing our emotions and adopting new habits that reflect who we are and want to be.

As emotional management is the core of our procrastination solution, so emotional management techniques are potentially the most impactful that you will use. These techniques may take longer to become habits, as they change a fundamental aspect of yourself. These deep, ingrained emotional habits can be changed but expect them to take longer to integrate into your life than simple time management habits.

Emotional Techniques

Set your goals and ask why

I'm sure you already have goals you want to achieve, but you must find out if there are any underlying emotional reasons for each.

For each of your goals, write down your goals and ask yourself 'why' for each. Keep asking why until you can't go any further. It might lead to a deeper understanding of yourself and your motivations. "I want to be wealthy" Why? "Because I want to feel secure". Why? "Because my parents argued a lot about money, and we couldn't afford much as a child."

Do you see how this might change your understanding of your motivations? This process might make some goals clearer and change others.

Make your reasons visible

It's easy to forget how important the reasons are your want to achieve your goals. So write them down, and put them somewhere you'll see every day. I use a sticky note on my monitor, and at the end of the day, I stick it right in the middle of the screen so it's the first thing I'll see tomorrow.

Make sure you see your goals every day.

Remember your future self

Suppose you think about your future self as a different person. In that case, it's easier to put off things that require effort — like saving for retirement or exercising regularly — because you're not going to benefit from them anyway. But suppose you focus on your future self being part of your current identity. In that case, it becomes harder to let yourself down later on when you finally do sit down at the computer and get started on that project or exercise session.

Pause, close your eyes, and picture yourself in the near future. Breathe and mentally tell your future self that you understand them and will do your best to support them, as you would help a close friend who is struggling.

Understand that your future self is part of you and deserves your compassion.

Change your self-talk

According to Boston College and the University of Houston researchers, self-talk can influence our behavior.

We all use an internal voice to give ourselves instructions, and it's a powerful tool. If we're not careful, our inner voice can become hostile and critical, making us feel terrible about ourselves. This leads us to procrastinate—we don't want to do anything because we don't think we're good enough!

Start a document, and on the left-hand side, make a list of the most common phrases you say to yourself. When I did this, I was so surprised - I was being exceedingly hard on myself, saying things I'd never say to anyone else.

On the right-hand side, make a list of things to say instead. Here are some of my own examples of what I was saying to myself and = what I changed it to.

- I'm an idiot = I'm working hard.
- I'm a failure = I'm succeeding, step by step.
- F*** this = I've got this.

This takes some work, but each time you catch yourself being negative, immediately say your positive phrase to overwrite your internal voice with a positive one.

You'll slowly see your mindset and strengthen and improve.

Change 'can't' to 'don't'

Another way to do this is to change the word 'cant' to 'don't' in your inner dialogues. If you tell yourself you *can't* do something, it sounds to your mind that you'd like to, but you're being held back from it by external circumstances.

On the other hand, saying '*don't*' is empowering - "I don't drink alcohol" or "I don't waste time" is better.

One study revealed that people working toward a fitness and health goal were likelier to commit harmful actions if they told themselves they couldn't. For instance, they were likelier to skip the gym or eat junk food if they told themselves they couldn't. However, when it came to those who used the "I can't" strategy, only one out of ten could resist these temptations.

Do the worst, first

Whichever task feels like the hardest one to do, do it first.

This is especially powerful when you can complete the 'worst' task as your first task in the morning. The rest of the day is better already! Do it first, get it over with, and unlock an immediate rush of energy. Brian Tracy calls this 'eating the frog'.

Don't move

Sometimes known by writers as the 'butt-in-chair' method.

Author Neil Gaiman uses this technique to write some of the best-selling fantasy stories in the world. When he writes, he writes in a gazebo in his garden where there are no distractions. He sits down and doesn't allow himself to move from that spot. He can look around, daydream, whatever he likes, except move. As there's no internet, no phone, and no distractions, eventually, he starts writing for something to do.

When in doubt, do

Sometimes you can feel confused and unsure about which course of action is best. You need more information when this happens, and you feel paralyzed by choice. You can only get more information by acting. So cut through the doubt, the fear, and the uncertainty by taking action and then reassessing later.

So start doing a task that will lead toward one of the outcomes. This will lead you to further insights and give you time to correct, if necessary.

Reward yourself

Don't treat yourself like a robot. When you achieve something good, healthily reward yourself. Choose a small reward that's meaningful, something you enjoy doing, and do it.

Be careful not to get thrown off course with large rewards that distract you and prevent you from your tasks again.

Get angry (in moderation)

If all else fails, anger can give you a burst of motivation to get started. Think about how angry not being able to achieve your goals makes you, how annoyed you are that you're procrastinating, and let that energy carry you forward into starting. Blast some high-energy music, and go for it!

A word of caution: use this sparingly, as it could backfire and be even more demotivating, plus it can sometimes break the rule of no negative self-talk.

Accept less than perfection

According to scientists, the most common cause of procrastination is analysis paralysis. This condition occurs when people become so focused on being a perfectionist that they don't take the time to think about other things.

A study conducted on professors revealed that those who are perfectionists are more likely to be less productive than those who are not perfectionists. The study's findings, published in 2010, provide important insight into the nature of perfectionism.[20]

Use momentum

Momentum is a powerful force, and you can use it to help you. The trick with momentum is to start with smaller tasks to give you an emotional win, use the feel-good energy released to propel you into the next task, and so on.

So decide on three smaller tasks you'd like to get done (ideally each will take less than 20 minutes). Vow to finish the first, no matter what. Start, and ignore everything until it's finished. High-five yourself, prepare the second task, then take ten minutes break. Repeat until all three tasks are done.

14

Mindset Management Techniques

"A small daily task, if it be really daily, will beat the labors of a spasmodic Hercules." - Anthony Trollope.

Your mindset is critically important to overcoming procrastination. Your mindset is your attitude towards your ability to learn and grow and specific tactics you can use to frame the way you work.

Doing all of this consistently trains your mind, like an athlete trains their body.

Procrastination is a problem that psychologists have studied for hundreds of years. The term was coined in the 1800s by a psychologist named Frederick William Novick[21]. The word means "putting off until tomorrow what should be done today," and it's estimated that up to 95% of people procrastinate at some point in their lives.

It will also give tips for developing better strategies for managing your mindset to get more done when it matters most.

Ask your future self

Develop a relationship with your future self. Build empathy with your future self by asking new persona - what would they want you to do? What would they thank you for doing now? How would they be different, be better because of you?

Visualize this briefly, for a minute or so, and you'll build a stronger connection, or better 'temporal thinking,' that we discussed in Chapter 4.

Develop a growth mindset

You've probably heard of the "growth mindset" from Carol Dweck —the idea that anyone can learn anything if they just put their mind to it, compared to a fixed mindset (where people believe their abilities are fixed)[22].

A growth mindset will help you persevere through the challenges of overcoming procrastination because it gives you the belief that you can improve if you do the work.

To develop a growth mindset, believe that you can grow and improve. What most others can do, you can do. If you find yourself having negative thoughts or not thinking an act is possible, challenge it and find the root cause. It'll almost always be an irrational belief you can overcome with the rest of these tips. And once you prove yourself capable over time, this negativity will occur less and less.

Visualize the process

Visualize the process, not the outcome that you want to achieve. Don't stop and think about each tedious step along the way, but focus on the outcome. Now start!

Researchers published a paper suggesting that positive visualization is in-effective and counterproductive[23]. They found that positive visualization of success resulted in the draining of energy and ambition. Heart rate decreases, blood pressure lowers, and our brain is tricked into thinking all is well in our mind's fantasy land of success. Time to kick back and relax!

In one study, the researchers showed that thirsty, water-deprived participants experienced an energy drain due to visualizing a glass of icy cold water. They also found that participants who were told to visualize succeeding at their goals throughout the week achieved significantly fewer goals than those told to think about the challenges they faced in any way they liked. Even more interesting is that the positive visualisers reported feeling less energetic than the other group—and physiological tests backed up these lethargic sentiments.

What's the next action?

David Allen dropped a phenomenal technique in his classic productivity book, 'Getting Things Done'. It's identifying what the very next physical action is.

Not sure what's next? Think about the very next physical action you need to take. What does it look like? Is it turning on your computer? Clicking a mouse to open a browser? Picking up the phone? What's next after that? Do it (don't think) and repeat.

This technique is best used with the next one, 'make it smaller':

Make it smaller

When you feel overwhelmed by a task, break it down into smaller pieces. Looking at a huge project is intimidating and will deter you. How do you eat an elephant? One bite at a time, as the old joke says.

To do so, ask yourself - what do you need to do to complete your task? If it's an essay, what's the word count? If it's a report, what are the sections? Once you know what that is, decide how long each section will take and divide your time accordingly.

Single focus

Close the browser tabs, clear a space, and move from multi-focus to single focus. Science has shown us that we can't multitask. Instead, we switch between single-tasking. Every time we switch tasks, it takes time and energy[24].

Eliminate, Automate, Delegate, or Outsource

If you can, simplify your work using one of these four tactics.

Eliminate - do you really need to do this? If you can get away with not doing it, remove it from your to-do list.

Automate - is it possible to automate the process? If you do repetitive tasks on a computer, see if it's possible to automate them.

Delegate - at work, can someone else help you with this? Are you doing someone else's work out of kindness? Can you ask your partner to help you with chores if they seem to be slacking? Re-allocate work where possible.

Outsource - get someone else to do it for you. Plenty of people are willing to help with almost any task on sites like Fiverr.com for a low fee.

Make yourself accountable

Ask someone to hold you accountable for your actions. Sites like stickK.com are one way to do this - you sign a contract for an agreed amount of money to ensure you complete the task. The referee will check if you've completed it, and if you haven't - your money gets donated to a good cause. You can even arrange for friends and family to cheer you on digitally. You can also ask friends and family to do this, which could lead to arguments!

Temptation Bundling

The concept of temptation bundling was created by Katy Milkman, a behavioral economist at the University of Pennsylvania[25]. It suggests that people should combine a behavior that's good for them in the long run with one they want to do in the short term.

For example, listening to podcasts when you do chores or reading when you commute to work. It's understandable why it works - you do an activity you like only when you do an activity you don't like. They 'cancel each other out'.

Have an internet break

Or better yet, remove your phone from view altogether! One study showed asked participants to perform a concentration test in one of four ways - with their smartphones either in their pockets, on their desks, locked drawers or removed from the room[26].

The results were significant — people's concentration was lowest the more in view the smartphone was, but increased the further away and out of sight it became. Concentration was 26% better when the smartphones were in a different room!

Use productive procrastination

Productive procrastination is doing something useful while procrastinating from a more critical task. For example, when you should be writing a dissertation, you might procrastinate by watering your plants, organizing your sock drawer, or tidying your bedroom.

While it's still procrastination, it's better to be productive than not. One way to use this to your advantage is to list small chores you need to do and do them if you can't avoid procrastinating. There's a fine line between taking a break and procrastinating.

Turn it into a game

Gamification is when you add elements of games into your workday. For example, if you're trying to write an article but keep getting distracted by your email notifications, try turning off all your notifications for a while and just focusing on writing for a set period. When that timer goes off, check your email as a reward for finishing your article!

Another way to gamify your work is by assigning yourself points every time you complete a project or reach an important goal at work (like sending out a newsletter). These points will keep track of how much progress you're making toward the goals you set for yourself at the beginning of the year—and they'll give you something else fun to focus on besides just getting through the day's tasks!

Get into flow

A flow state is when our brain fully engages in an activity, and all our attention is focused on that activity. Think of it like being so engrossed in what you're doing that the rest of the world fades away—you forget about time passing or needing food or water—and in this state, we tend to be more productive (and happier).

So how do we get into flow? It's simple: set yourself up for success by choosing a challenging project to stimulate your brain but not so hard that it overwhelms it; give yourself enough time and space to focus, and then get started! Once you're in a flow state, all those distractions will melt away, and nothing else will matter except getting down whatever it is

15

Environmental Techniques

It's surprising how much our environments can impact our ability to overcome procrastination. In our modern world, we have two environments that we spend our time in - physical and digital.

Our physical surroundings include our body and how it interacts with what's around us. Our digital environment consists of all we do online and with our technology.

You can use these techniques to organize your physical and digital worlds better. It's incredible how a few simple tweaks to our environment can make us feel refreshed and give us more energy to overcome procrastination.

Physical Techniques

Better physical posture

It's amazing what such a simple change can make to your outlook, focus, and feeling—simply sitting or standing up straight, with your shoulders back and with proper posture, you signal to your brain that now is the time to feel energized and focused.

Your brain and body are connected - improve one, and the other follows. On the other hand, if you're slouching, it sends a message that it's downtime, time to relax and not get things done.

Breathe properly

Oxygen is fuel for our bodies and brains.

When stressed out or anxious, our breathing tends to be shallow—we take quick, shallow breaths that don't fill our lungs with much oxygen. This can cause many problems: blood flow is restricted to certain parts of the body (like muscles), which means less oxygen is getting to your brain and other organs that need it.

If you're not taking deep breaths, your body will feel short on energy and under stress. It's hard to think clearly when you're feeling like this. It's also hard to get through tasks if you're worried about how much energy you have left in the tank!

There are many benefits to breathing correctly:

- It makes you feel more relaxed.
- Improves your concentration and focus.
- It helps you sleep better at night.

It also gives you the energy to do your work, feel energized, and are less likely to procrastinate.

When you breathe deeply, you're giving your brain and body the oxygen it needs to function at its best.

Leverage peak-energy times

Do your most complex tasks when you have the most energy.

This tactic involves being aware of when you have the most energy. You probably have a gut feeling of when this is already, but try noting when you feel tired and energized over the next week. Once you know your energy pattern, try and schedule your most challenging tasks for when you have the most energy.

Guard your energy carefully. Make sure you get 7-8 hours of sleep a night. Do your most important tasks when you have the most energy. Finally, guard your energy against energy-sucking events and people wherever possible.

Take a break

You start to slow down when you've been productive for too long. Tasks that took 20 minutes now take an hour or longer. It's time to change scenery (and if you use a screen, to give your eyes a break).

Although we're all unique, we all need to take a break. How often and how long will depend on your circumstances, but take one regularly. A good idea is to combine this with the time management suggestions in the next chapter. Bonus tip: go outside when you take a break. Even for five minutes, fresh air will reinvigorate you.

Reduce friction

Make sure what you need is close at hand.

Whatever tools you need, organize your workspace, so everything is to hand.

There's nothing worse than having to stop midway through a task to have to go and find a tool you need.

Organize and remove clutter

Feelings of overwhelm can be magnified by the amount of clutter you see.

This is why it's essential to remove any visual distractions. This means getting rid of clutter and unnecessary items. If you're working at home, this can be easier said than done because we tend to accumulate things that don't help us with our work.

You're more likely to feel overwhelmed and distracted when your environment is cluttered. When stressed out in a messy space, it's hard to focus on one thing. Clutter can also be a physical manifestation of your inner thoughts. If clutter makes you feel anxious or depressed, then getting rid of it could help alleviate some of the negative emotions associated with procrastination.

Bring in nature.

Use natural lighting. The best way to overcome procrastination is to bring in nature. Having natural light in your workspace can help reduce stress and make you feel more relaxed.

Put plants in your office. Plants help improve air quality and give a room a great aesthetic that can boost productivity and creativity, ultimately increasing your mood!

Have a view of nature from where you work every day. Having views of nature from where you work helps create an environment conducive to focus and concentration, so having a window that looks out onto trees or other vegetation outside can be highly beneficial!

Digital Environment

The digital age has made it easier than ever for us to procrastinate. Our phones and computers constantly distract us from what we need to get done, from emails to social media notifications. When these distractions are continually vying for our attention, they make it hard for us to focus and get things done efficiently.

In a time when we're constantly being bombarded with new information and opportunities, it's easy to get distracted and overwhelmed. We might have more options than ever, but we also have more distractions. The good news is that there are ways to improve your digital environment so that it's more conducive to productivity and less conducive to procrastination. Here's how:

Put your phone on silent.

The urge to check for new messages is overwhelming at times.

If this is the case for you, put your phone on silent (or turn off notifications) when working on important tasks. You may also want to consider putting your phone in another room while working on projects that require concentration and focus. If even this seems too difficult for you, avoid checking it during breaks and at night before bedtime; these are two times when many people spend more time on their phones than any other part of the day.

Set a Gatekeeper

Limit yourself to specific websites at specific times during the day (or week). This will help you avoid getting caught up in rabbit holes of browsing online when you only want one quick answer from Google!

Search online for 'browser extensions' that will allow you to block websites that you find tempting. You can set times and dates that you're allowed to view them. All other times, if you try and visit them, it won't let you. tk provide?

Organize your files and bookmarks

If your project files are messy, it'll add friction and mental stress to your work day. Not being able to find a critical file is incredibly frustrating and will likely cause you to rage-quit your project and procrastinate for the rest of the day. So take time to organize these, and you'll thank yourself later.

Bonus tip: clean up these files as you use them, and do a quick check once a week in a weekly review.

16

Time Management Techniques

"We all sorely complain of the shortness of time and yet have much more than we know what to do with. Our lives are either spent in doing nothing at all, or in doing nothing to the purpose, or in doing nothing that we ought to do. We are always complaining that our days are few, and acting as though there would be no end of them."

- Seneca

These techniques are simple and highly practical, but their role in beating procrastination shouldn't be underestimated. Implementing all of these will have you getting things done fast and moving you towards your ideal self.

Learn to prioritize

Prioritizing is an essential time management skill. It helps you decide what's most important and focus your energy on one task at a time. To prioritize, you must know what will make the most significant difference in your life. Ask yourself:

- What will make the most significant impact on my life?
- Which projects or tasks will benefit me most?

- Which tasks can be done quickly and easily?
- What things are most urgent and need to be done right now?

Hold a weekly review

Hold a weekly meeting with only yourself. The goal of this meeting is to review your week and plan for the coming week. This concept can be life-changing - it's a regular time to check in with yourself and see how you're doing and your progress with your goals. Make it a fun time, choose a quiet time (Sunday mornings or evenings are ideal), and ask yourself these questions:

- What went well this last week? What could I have done better?
- How am I progressing against my goals?
- What do I want to get done next week?

Set deadlines

deadline serves as an internal motivator, which helps you stay focused on the task.

Set a deadline for yourself: This is important because you need to know when something has to be done to plan and assign tasks in order of importance. If more than one project requires completion by this date, prioritize them based on what needs attention most urgently (e.g., school work before personal errands).

Set a deadline for your team members: Setting deadlines for each member will ensure that everyone knows when they need to get their part done, so they don't end up being late with their deliverables—and it prevents any last-minute scrambling in case they run into problems along the way.

Schedule time blocks

To start, schedule blocks of time for each task. If you're writing a book, schedule a block of time to write your next chapter. Then, when it's time to work on that chapter, clear away all distractions and focus on getting the words down—figuratively speaking, of course. Once that block is done, take a short break (maybe five minutes) before moving on to your next block of time for writing.

If you have an appointment or meeting coming up in your calendar and it requires some preparation—say an interview or presentation—make sure you've scheduled enough time before the event so that there isn't pressure to rush through it at the last minute (or worse yet forget about it altogether). And once again: keep all distractions out from this period so that when it's done and over with (and hopefully successful), you can move forward feeling good about what just happened!

Schedule free time

The key to overcoming procrastination is to set aside time for yourself. That doesn't mean you should be afraid of taking a break; you need to make time for the things necessary to you and your well-being, whether going to the gym, reading a book, or even spending time with friends and family.

Don't feel guilty about taking care of yourself. Your health is essential; nothing else will get done if you don't care for yourself! If this means giving up something that is not essential, then so be it. There's no point being stressed over work when there are more important things in life!

Log your time.

One of the best ways to get a handle on your time is to log it. You can use a time tracker, a time management tool, or simply keep a diary. If you're unsure where your day goes, try keeping track of how long you spend on any given task. That way, when you find yourself procrastinating, you'll have the evidence needed to make a change.

Learn to say no

Learn to say no and prioritize your own needs. If you say yes to every request from your boss or a friend, you'll never have time for yourself. Don't feel like you have to be nice always; sometimes, saying no is the best thing for everyone involved.

Do two minutes

Keep clutter at bay with the two-minute rule. If a new obligation or task comes into your life, and it will take less than two minutes - do it now. You'll feel so much better, and it will keep clutter and overwhelm at bay.

Set a timer (1) - Pomodoro method

This method is a classic and one you may already be familiar with. The idea is to work in 25-minute bursts (known as a Pomodoro) and take a 5-minute break between each Pomodoro.

A great way to use this technique is by using a built-in timer app on your phone, which allows you to set timers for different tasks.

Set a timer (2) - The "(10+2)x5" method

In this method, you set a timer and work on a task for 10 minutes straight. Then, you rest for 2 minutes. You repeat this pattern five times, so it's called the "(10+2)x5" method.

The idea behind this is that even if you don't feel like working or are tempted to procrastinate, as soon as your timer goes off and tells you it's time to take a break, your brain will start looking forward to getting back into the groove of things again—giving yourself permission to do some mindless scrolling on social media or check email can be just enough of an excuse not to get started with your work again! This technique helps reduce guilt about taking breaks when needed and also helps prevent burnout from working too long without a break.

Ivy Lee Method

One of the most effective productivity systems I have found is the Ivy Lee Method. It has six steps.

At the end of the workday, write down six tasks you need to complete the next day. When you get to work tomorrow, focus on the first task. Then, start working on the second one. Follow the same strategy throughout the day. At the end of the day, remove any unfinished items from your list and put them in a new one for the following day. Repeat.

17

Turning Techniques into Habits

The last four chapters have given you all the techniques you need to get to zero procrastination.

However, trying to implement all of them at once would lead to cognitive overload - if you try to change everything at once, there's a good chance that nothing will change at all—you'll get overwhelmed and give up too soon!

So what's the best way to use them effectively and as quickly as possible?

This is where we need to turn to the science of habit creation. Habits are automatic actions, done almost without thinking. They are triggered by something, and they get stronger with repetition. Let's look at a process to develop the techniques into permanent habits.

Start slowly

Choose one technique you'd like to implement first. If you're feeling ambitious, choose Focus on one thing at a time and make sure it sticks. That way, when other habits follow suit later on, they'll feel more natural because of their association with the previous success rate achieved through this initial routine-building effort.

Start stacking habits

Create a productive routine that flows from one activity to another.

You probably already have a routine that is a series of habits, one after another. Your morning routine probably involves going to the bathroom, brushing your teeth, having a shower, getting dressed, and eating breakfast. Each habit is triggered by the end of the previous one.

Choose a technique from a previous chapter, and add it to the end of a habit you already have. Wait until it's a habit, add a new habit to the end, and repeat!

It's helpful to build up effective morning, lunchtime, and evening routines with this method.

Identify Your Procrastination Trigger

The first step to breaking the cycle is identifying when you procrastinate. Is there a specific time of day? A particular emotion you feel? Or when a specific situation occurs? What's your trigger?

If you know what sets off your procrastination, it's easier to figure out how to avoid that trigger in the future. Maybe it's boredom, or perhaps it's an emotional reaction to something else. Whatever it is, try to figure out what sets you off so that you can be more aware of your actions next time.

Track your progress

Tracking your progress is a great way to stay motivated. If you're trying to lose weight, it can help you see how many pounds you've lost over time and identify areas that need improvement (i.e., if you've been exercising more but haven't been eating as well).

There are many ways to track your progress: a journal, spreadsheet, or app. You might want to write down what you ate and how much sleep you got each day; keep tabs on your moods; record how long it took for an errand or task; note how productive various tasks were for the week, and so on.

Be kind

Don't beat yourself up if you mess up and fall off the wagon. Just plan to get back on track and start fresh as soon as possible. Don't feel guilty or be too hard on yourself; dust yourself off and start again.

Be aware of your emotions

Pay attention to your feelings about the habit.

You may feel excited, nervous, fearful, frustrated - remember that's not you, it's just a feeling. It will pass. Remember, you can do your target technique regardless of which emotion you're feeling at that moment.

It's also ok to be compassionate with yourself if you mess up. You're human, so don't expect to hit the technique 100% of the time right out of the gate.

Conclusion

Hopefully, these tips will help you to turn your habits into routines. Remember that it's not about being perfect all the time but instead making a commitment to yourself and sticking with it. If you fall off the wagon, get back on track! Remember that it takes consistent practice over time for new behaviors to become second nature. Find a supportive community of like-minded people who can help keep each other motivated and hold each other accountable.

18

Recap

We're all fighting procrastination in our own way.

It can be a painful, frustrating, and depressing fight. Understanding the causes of procrastination and having a solid roadmap on how. Hopefully, this book has thrown some light on tk

We learned that procrastination is an emotional issue, which includes how we think about our future selves. It's not that we're lazy, incompetent, or a failure. We can all escape from the clutches of procrastination by learning how to manage our emotions and use proven techniques.

We learned that we can arrange those management techniques into categories - emotional, mindset, environmental, and time management. Doing so allows us to work on different areas as we need to, in the most beneficial order.

We learned the techniques themselves, their categories, and why they work.
We also learned how to turn these techniques into habits, so we can integrate them into our lives and innoculate ourselves against procrastination again.

By doing so, you'll be able to reach 'procrastination zero'. Sure, you'll take breaks, relax, and have downtime. But it will be a pleasurable time, not time spent feeling guilty that you should be doing something more important.

Lastly (and perhaps most importantly), we learned to treat ourselves with care, compassion, and forgiveness. Changing yourself is complex, and there may be times when you fall back to your old habits when you're tired or stressed. However, you now have the knowledge and experience to use as a reference to restart if you need to.

I wish you all the best in your journey and a life where you reach your potential.

Notes

YOU'RE NOT ALONE

1 Stanley, Julian. 'Four Steps to Building Your Wellbeing'. *SecEd* 2015, no. 22 (10 September 2015). https://doi.org/10.12968/sece.2015.22.12a.

2 Steel, Piers. 'The Nature of Procrastination: A Meta-Analytic and Theoretical Review of Quintessential Self-Regulatory Failure'. *Psychological Bulletin* 133 (2007): 65–94. https://doi.org/10.1037/0033-2909.133.1.65.

THE PRICE OF PROCRASTINATION

3 Steel, Piers. 'The Nature of Procrastination: A Meta-Analytic and Theoretical Review of Quintessential Self-Regulatory Failure'. *Psychological Bulletin* 133 (2007): 65–94. https://doi.org/10.1037/0033-2909.133.1.65.

4 Nguyen, Brenda, Piers Steel, and Joseph R. Ferrari. 'Procrastination's Impact in the Workplace and the Workplace's Impact on Procrastination'. *International Journal of Selection and Assessment* 21, no. 4 (2013): 388–99. https://doi.org/10.1111/ijsa.12048.

5 Nguyen, Brenda, Piers Steel, and Joseph R. Ferrari. 'Procrastination's Impact in the Workplace and the Workplace's Impact on Procrastination'. *International Journal of Selection and Assessment* 21, no. 4 (2013): 388–99. https://doi.org/10.1111/ijsa.12048.

6 Sunstein, 'Empirically Informed Regulation'.

THE ROOTS OF PROCRASTINATION

7 Sirois and Pychyl, 'Procrastination and the Priority of Short-Term Mood Regulation'.

8 Steel and König, 'Integrating Theories of Motivation'.

EMOTIONS RUNNING WILD

9 Clark et al., 'Tribalism Is Human Nature'.

10 'Insufficient Task-outcome Association Promotes Task Procrastination through a Decrease of Hippocampal–Striatal Interaction'.

11 'The Nature of Procrastination: A Meta-Analytic and Theoretical Review of Quintessential Self-Regulatory Failure. - PsycNET'. Accessed 17 September 2022. https://psycnet.apa.org/doiLanding?doi=10.1037%2F0033-2909.133.1.65.

12 Dolan, 'Just Having Your Cell Phone in Your Possession Can Impair Your Learning, Study Suggests'.

13 'Insufficient Task-outcome Association Promotes Task Procrastination through a Decrease of Hippocampal–Striatal Interaction'.

14 Abbasi and Alghamdi, 'The Prevalence, Predictors, Causes, Treatment, and Implications of Procrastination Behaviors in General, Academic, and Work Setting'.

TYPES OF PROCRASTINATION

15 Rozental, Alexander, Erik Forsell, Andreas Svensson, David Forsström, Gerhard Andersson, and Per Carlbring. 'Differentiating Procrastinators from Each Other: A Cluster Analysis'. *Cognitive Behaviour Therapy* 44, no. 6 (2 November 2015): 480–90. https://doi.org/10.1080/16506073.2015.1059353.

HOW WE PROCRASTINATE

16 'Therapeutic Benefits of Laughter in Mental Health: A Theoretical Review'.

17 Kroese, Floor M., Sanne Nauts, Bart A. Kamphorst, Joel H. Anderson, and Denise T. D. de Ridder. 'Chapter 5 - Bedtime Procrastination: A Behavioral Perspective on Sleep Insufficiency'. In *Procrastination, Health, and Well-Being*, edited by Fuschia M. Sirois and Timothy A. Pychyl, 93–119. San Diego: Academic Press, 2016. https://doi.org/10.1016/B978-0-12-802862-9.00005-0.

18 'Peter M Gollwitzer'.

CONCEPT #3: THINKING

19 Sweller, John. 'Cognitive Load during Problem Solving: Effects on Learning'. *Cognitive Science* 12, no. 2 (1 April 1988): 257–85. https://doi.org/10.1016/0364-0213(88)90023-7.

EMOTIONAL MANAGEMENT TECHNIQUES

20 "Perfectionism dimension and research productivity in Psychology Professors: Implications for understanding the (mal)adaptiveness of perfectionism" Canadian Journal of Behavioral Science, October 2010

MINDSET MANAGEMENT TECHNIQUES

21 Rothblum, Solomon, and Murakami, 'Affective, Cognitive, and Behavioral Differences between High and Low Procrastinators'.

22 'Carol Dweck Revisits the "Growth Mindset" - Education Week'.

23 Kappes and Oettingen, 'The Emergence of Goal Pursuit'.

24 Rubinstein, Meyer, and Evans, 'Executive Control of Cognitive Processes in Task Switching'.

25 Milkman, Minson, and Volpp, 'Holding the Hunger Games Hostage at the Gym'.

26 Racism et al., 'Does Smartphone Use Effect Your Anxiety And Depression?'

Made in United States
Troutdale, OR
12/18/2023